THE HISTORY AND TECHNIQUES
OF THE GREAT MASTERS

TOULOUSE-LAUTREC

THE HISTORY AND TECHNIQUES
OF THE GREAT MASTERS

TOULOUSE-LAUTREC

Christopher Ackroyd

TIGER BOOKS INTERNATIONAL
LONDON

A QUARTO BOOK

This edition published by
Tiger Books International Ltd
3, Friars Lane,
Richmond,
Surrey, TW9 1NL

ISBN 1 85501 011 9

This book was designed and produced by
Quarto Publishing plc
The Old Brewery, 6 Blundell Street
London N7 9BH

Project Editor Hazel Harrison
Designer Carole Perks
Picture Researcher Katherine Russell-Cobb

Art Director Moira Clinch
Editorial Director Carolyn King

Typeset by Aptimage Limited
22 Clinton Place, Seaford, East Sussex BN25 1NP
Manufactured in Hong Kong by Regent
Publishing Services Limited
Printed in Hong Kong by Leefung-Asco
Printers Ltd

CONTENTS

THE PAINTINGS

INTRODUCTION

Photograph of Henri de
Toulouse-Lautrec (detail)
Date unknown

"At last, I looked Lautrec straight in the eyes. Oh, how fine, large, richly warm and astonishingly, luminously bright they were! I kept on gazing into them and suddenly Lautrec became aware of it and took his spectacles off. He knew his one magnificent feature and he offered it to me with all his generosity. And his gesture showed me his ludicrous, dwarfish little hand, which was so square and attached to extraordinarily short marionettish arms."

This was how the cabaret singer Yvette Guilbert remembered the first of many meetings with Henri de Toulouse-Lautrec. She was not the only one to be won over by the performance of vivacity and wit that deflected attention from his deformity. However, she was more perceptive than some in recognizing so quickly the tragedy behind the eyes. And she was to show a creditable lack of vanity in her realization that the drawings he did of her were not mere representations.

Both were famous by the time he began to work from her, and she ignored the opposition of her various friends and advisors, only mildly reproving him for his most outrageous distortions. Her stage persona was itself a kind of caricature, a medium for satire and innuendo by which she deflated social pretensions and hypocrisy. The ends of artist and performer were thus compatible, Lautrec's primary purpose being an analysis of personality, more particularly of those aspects of human nature revealed when behavioural niceties are discarded. More than any other artist of this period he chose to operate in the seedy areas shared by polite society — the *monde* — and its vulgar counterpart — the *demi-monde,* wilfully specializing in the world of prostitutes, petty crooks, *roués* and the fashionable men who moved imperturbably among them. To some extent Lautrec shared the latter's air of detached observation, but his engagement was more pronounced — his gleeful bohemianism caused his early death at the age of thirty-six. Ironically, his lifestyle has led him to be identified with the romantic notion of *fin de siècle* gaiety. But although his art does in some ways encapsulate an exuberant period on which Paris still capitalizes, it frequently strikes a note of cautionary melancholy that makes it ultimately impossible to define as either simply characteristic of the milieu or as his own peculiarly private view.

Early life

Lautrec's separateness, the quality that pervades so many of his paintings, was materially affected by the circumstances of his childhood. He was born in 1864 at Albi in south-west France, an aristocrat in a century when the majority of effective power was increasingly controlled by the middle classes. His quixotic father, Count Alphonse-Charles de Toulouse-Lautrec-Monfa, seems to have charged through life from one eccentric gesture to the next, his extravagant adventures outdoing even those of his son in his later, drink deranged years.

Although neither he nor his parents were aware of it, Henri suffered from a bone deficiency, quite possibly the result of inbreeding. This was aggravated by the onset of puberty, with its sudden acceleration of growth, and when he broke both thighs in two successive years, each the result of an unspectacular fall, the bones failed to join up properly. The result was that his legs stopped growing, although his torso and head were of normal proportions, and his full adult height was only five feet (152.4cm). When it became clear that the accidents that caused his son's misshapeness would preclude him from a life devoted mainly to horses and hunting, the count ceased to take an active interest in Henri's development. He and his wife were largely estranged, maintaining little more than a marriage of appearances, and thus the supervision of the boy's upbringing fell almost entirely to his mother, the Countess Adèle, who withdrew him from school to undergo a variety of cures.

He met his misfortunes with a natural buoyancy of spirit that was to remain as the core of the charm he

HENRI DE TOULOUSE-LAUTREC
Viaduct of Castel-Vieil at Albi
1880, Musée Toulouse-Lautrec, Albi

Lautrec rarely painted landscapes, declaring once that "only the figure exists," and that nature should be no more than background. This early work was painted from the balcony of the Hôtel du Bôsc, one of several country estates in south-west France owned by Lautrec's family. It is typical of the broadly impressionistic manner he developed before his formal artistic training in Paris.

exerted in later life. Lautrec always disdained self-pity, and even more so the pity of others. One of his most characteristic responses to some setback in adult life was to rasp, "It's of no consequence." Surviving letters to friends and cousins written during the convalescence from his accidents reveal an amazing degree of humour and courage.

Early training

Lautrec had shown a talent for drawing before the accidents. Had they not occurred this would probably have remained at the level of a cultivated hobby, as it was for one of his uncles, Charles. Even Lautrec's father, the count, occasionally attended classes run by a specialist in equestrian subjects, René Princeteau, and visits to this artist's studio in the Rue du Faubourg-St-Honoré constituted Lautrec's first introduction to the professional art world. The enforced sedentary life of the convalescent was made slightly more tolerable by the ability to focus his energy on the skills that remained accessible to him. His earliest efforts reflect his family background and interests: thoroughbred horses, hounds and hawks, fre-

HENRI DE TOULOUSE-LAUTREC
The Four-in-Hand
1881, Musée du Petit Palais, Paris

Spirited horses were one of the main passions of Lautrec's father, here represented driving a coach along the Promenade des Anglais, Nice. Equestrian subjects not unnaturally predominate in Lautrec's early work. In theme and style this example reflects the influence of his earliest teacher, Princeteau, but the vigorous brushwork used to depict movement presages his mature manner.

LEON BONNAT
The Decapitation of Saint Denis
1885, Panthéon, Paris

Lautrec studied only briefly under Bonnat, but during the early 1880s he tried hard to discipline his style according to the academic precepts on which a painting of this kind was based. It is an interesting coincidence that Bonnat situated the execution outside the Roman Temple of Mars, on the hill of Montmartre, the very district that was to provide Lautrec with so many subjects of so very different a character.

quently in vigorous motion, and painted in an appropriately boisterous style. By the mid 1880s he had largely abandoned this kind of subject matter, and his tastes were becoming decidedly urban, but he never lost this early ability to capture rapidly the essentials of brisk movement. Strangely, animal themes were to recur in the final years when alcoholic excess had brought him to physical and nervous collapse. These later works are less directly observed and were the products of imagination and memory, as if he were harking back to a period of relatively unsullied optimism.

Princeteau became increasingly impressed by the precocious ease with which his "studio foster child" assimilated his own manner. He was aware too that Lautrec needed and would benefit from more rigorous tuition, and it was arranged that the young man should enter the *atelier* of the academician, Léon Bonnat. In May 1882, a month or so after his commencement, Lautrec reported the comments of his "majestic" new master: "Your painting isn't bad — it's clever, but it still isn't bad — but your drawing is simply atrocious." This opinion is revealing: the essence of Lautrec's painting style is his drawing, but not in the academic sense that Bonnat would have comprehended. The basis of the orthodox system of art training to which Lautrec submitted, first under Bonnat and then, from 1883, with Fernand Cormon, was a respect for classical sculpture and the masters of the High Renaissance. More immediately, it depended on precepts and methods stemming in France from the "School of David" at the beginning of the century. These were perpetuated by the Ecole des Beaux-Arts (where Bonnat became a professor and later director), and the results were annually displayed in their hundreds at the Paris Salon.

Bonnat eventually became a fierce opponent of all modern tendencies in art, and seems to have developed a special dislike of his former pupil. Four years after Lautrec's death he used his considerable influence to get the Commission of National Museums to revoke its decision to accept one of Lautrec's finest portraits, *Monsieur Delaporte at the Jardin de Paris*. Bonnat's style as a painter of grand historical subjects can be gauged from his contribution to the prestigious series of murals for the Panthéon in 1885. But his international reputation was as a painter of portraits, in which powerful realization of character was in part due to a forceful, almost bravura application of paint. Even more relevant to the formation of Lautrec's mature style was Bonnat's recognized brilliance in the rapid execution of oil sketches, both for copies from Old Masters and from the life model, and pupils of the equally conservative Cormon similarly spoke of his encouragement of swift informal copying in the Louvre.

In the second half of the 19th century it was not unusual to find progressive artists incorporating elements of their training into their mature styles. Whistler, for example, made a principle of the importance Charles Gleyre, his teacher, had attached to working from memory, and built a whole aesthetic credo on Gleyre's practice of arranging a picture's colour harmonies on the palette before touching the canvas. But the principal purpose of art teaching was to prepare students for entry into the Ecole des Beaux-Arts, and this was probably Lautrec's intention initially; certainly it was the course his family expected him to follow.

But in the early 1880s a number of new ideas were beginning to emerge in the wake of Impressionism, which was itself still controversial. Such developments were keenly discussed in the teaching studios, exacerbating the sense of disenchantment with traditional notions of art practice. In 1886 some of Cormon's students became so openly critical of his methods that he closed the studio, reopening a little later after expelling the worst offenders. (One of these was Emile Bernard, who was introduced to Gauguin at Pont-Aven later in the year.) Lautrec, who three years earlier had found Cormon's teaching insufficiently taxing, was not among the rebels, though he was by now of the same opinion. For two years, since he had taken a studio in Montmartre, he had been attending Cormon's less regularly, and his style had begun to change. He continued for a time to use the sombre tones and orthodox compositions encouraged by his official teachers, but gradually his naturally vivacious style began to reassert itself in themes redolent of his new surroundings.

Montmartre

In the 18th century, Montmartre, then a village outside Paris, was already known for its cheap taverns, drunkenness and licentiousness. Early in the following century, attracted by low rents and rural picturesqueness, artists began to gather there, along with writers, intellectuals and political malcontents. Through the century it was gradually transformed from a windmill-dotted, hill-top

HENRI DE TOULOUSE-LAUTREC
The Flirt — the Englishman Warrener at The Moulin Rouge
1892, Musée Toulouse-Lautrec, Albi

This is one of Lautrec's earliest colour lithographs, showing his grasp of the bold pictorial possibilities of Japanese art when combined with his naturally swift draughtsmanship. Large irregular areas of unmodulated colour and tone were partly responsible for the success of the poster designs he had begun to produce the year before, and the confidence he gained in this way began to bear fruit in his paintings also.

HENRI DE TOULOUSE-LAUTREC
The Chestnut Vendor
1897, Bibliothèque Nationale, Paris

Lautrec was an aristocrat, but paradoxically this, combined with his physical condition, enabled him to identify with the anti-bourgeois sentiments of people such as Aristide

Bruant and the graphic artist Steinlen. Overtly proletarian themes, such as this, however, were rare, and his use of the small dog (a frequent metaphor for his own physique) suggests that there may have been a symbolic intent in this unusually atmospheric drawing.

village to a densely populated, lower-class suburb; between 1830 and 1886 the estimated population rose from 6,000 to over 200,000. That it had continued its unsavoury character is apparent from a *Baedeker* entry for 1888: "The best cafés [in the centre of Paris] may with propriety be visited by ladies, but those on the north side of the Boulevards Montmartre and des Italiens should be avoided, as the society there is far from select."

Lautrec very quickly felt at home in Montmartre, and became identified with some of its notable performers. The first of these relationships was with the satirical singer Aristide Bruant, whose songs expressed his disdain for the fashionable toffs out slumming. Lautrec had begun to publish drawings in this vein in 1886, and had accumulated a significant body of illustrations before 1891, when his fame was immediately established through his poster designs, the first commissioned for the newly opened dance hall, the Moulin Rouge. A year later he began to produce fine lithographs, *The English-man Warrener at the Moulin Rouge* being one of his earliest essays in the medium to which he was to contribute a wealth of innovatory ideas and techniques. Friendship with Bruant was a crucial phase in

HENRI DE TOULOUSE-LAUTREC
Yvette Guilbert-Pessima
1898, British Museum, London

Lautrec specialized in depictions of popular entertainers. Sometimes (as with May Belfort or Loïe Fuller) his enthusiasm was short-lived, but he worked

consistently from both Yvette Guilbert and Jane Avril over a number of years, his depictions reflecting sustained friendships. Here he has caught the jaunty knowingness of the singer's mobile face with a minimum of lines.

Lautrec's education, as so much of his subsequent painting and graphic work was dependent on the brilliant realization of the characters of popular entertainers and of the varied types that made up their audiences. His first exhibited works were hung on the walls of Bruant's cabaret Le Mirliton and featured, for example, the singer himself and the riotous dancing of the "naturalistic quadrille" (the predecessor of the can-can) at the Elysée-Montmartre.

Thus, at the age of only twenty-one, Lautrec had already been seduced away from the career in the official art world that his family would have wished for him. His decisive rejection of academicism suggests a degree of certainty about his abilities, but there are indications that throughout his life he was unsure of his artistic stature in relation to the painters he most admired, notably Degas. His family wealth removed the pressure to earn a living from his art that many of his peers felt, and although he clearly had determination, it was not backed by any strong theoretical motivation, as Bernard's was. Nor did he have the sense of great purpose shown by Van Gogh, who had arrived in Paris in 1886 and also studied at Cormon's *atelier*.

Influences

Lautrec avoided attachment to any particular avant-garde group, but he was responsive to some of the leading ideas filtering through his network of acquaintances. Impressionism was clearly an influence on him, lightening and brightening his palette and loosening his brushwork, but his mature works are only minimally analyses of light, which was the main preoccupation of the Impressionists. He also benefited from the notion — not unique to the Impressionists — of sketch-like spontaneity as an equivalent for individuality and self expression. Several of his friends experimented seriously, if briefly, with variants of Seurat's Pointillism, and some of Lautrec's work of the early 1890s also suggests an interest, though the application of dots of colour was much looser and less "scientifically" based than that of the Neo-Impressionists. One of the most obvious stylistic influences is that of Van Gogh, which can be seen in Lautrec's own version of directional brushstrokes, creating a sense of three-dimensional form and space by means of linear striations and cross-hatching. But the painter to whom Lautrec owed most, both in terms of subject matter and technique, was Degas, who was a neighbour between 1887 and 1893. Like Degas, Lautrec experimented with pigment thinned with turpentine, and both artists made use of unconventional supports

EDGAR DEGAS
Café-concert at The Ambassadeurs
c 1875-7, Musée des Beaux-Arts, Lyon

Lautrec was keenly appreciative of Japanese art, but his adaptation of oriental compositional devices was at least as much due to his admiration for Degas. The critic Gustave Geffroy, writing on Lautrec, coined the term "human landscape." This is equally applicable to Degas who, as here, provided Lautrec with a scheme for combining stage performers and their audience.

such as unprimed canvas or brown cardboard, which absorbed the paint and gave a matt quality.

As early as 1882 Lautrec had recorded an enthusiasm for Japanese art, a taste shared by many artists of the period, and this led him in time, in paintings such as *Woman at her Toilet* (see page 47), to adopt compositional devices like oblique or elevated viewpoints to give enhanced immediacy to his compositions. This influence is particularly evident in his graphic work; knowledge of Japanese prints, as well as suggesting subjects, encouraged a bold and often asymmetrical disposition of forms; sharp overlapping of figures indicating brief momentary glimpses; and figures and objects cut off dramatically at the picture's edges — devices that Degas also used extensively.

Large, flat areas of colour were another feature of Japanese art that painters like Gauguin and Bernard incorporated into their work. Lautrec only rarely used these in his painting — his abstractions were always modified by naturalism — but it was an approach eminently suited to posters and lithographs, in which he was able to exploit simplicity of means even more than in his paintings. This was largely because he accepted the limitations of whatever medium he was working in. For example, he quickly realized the positive nature of blank areas of paper as a foil for the brilliant irregularities of his line, and in such works as *The Englishman Warrener at the Moulin Rouge* he plays off unbroken non-naturalistic areas against atmospheric, textured ones. Although visually this effect is quite different from the styles he was pursuing in his paintings, they too always combine touches of visual realism (usually faces and hands) within a sketchy context whose abstraction is stressed through clearly defined brushstrokes, unpainted ground and unmodulated colour.

Lautrec in context

Just as Lautrec had no fixed allegiance to any particular artistic group, his links with the avant-garde critics seem not to have been due to shared aesthetic ideals. For

example, two important advocates of Neo-Impressionism and Symbolism, Edouard Dujardin and Félix Fénéon, occur among the *dramatis personae* of Lautrec's paintings, but apart from some youthful allegories, the closest Lautrec came to Symbolism was in the later, sometimes nightmarish, works induced by extreme alcoholism and the effects of withdrawal. Closest to him theoretically were writers like Gustave Geffroy, who promoted the principles of Naturalism, but Lautrec's brand of sometimes bitter realism was less a matter of theory than of instinct and sympathy. When he began to exhibit with the progressive society *Les Vingt* in Brussels in 1888, the often favourable reception he had from such writers was probably partly due to his being recognized as a follower of Degas, and it was the latter's opinion that in many ways mattered to him most.

Lautrec's own politics were vaguely right-wing, and espousal by Anarchist reviewers may have caused him some amusement. However, their interpretation of his work was understandable in view of the evident humanitarian qualities of his depictions of the humbler inhabitants of Montmartre. Above all, it is within the broad context of Naturalism that his art is best understood as a significant contribution beyond purely personal observation. The poet Charles Baudelaire had urged painters to extract the age's "epic quality from the life of today and make us see and understand ... how great and poetic we are in our cravats and our patent leather boots." But he well understood that epic poetry requires a bond between heroism and tragedy. Writers like Flaubert and Zola elaborated on this ambiguity, and it is present too in Lautrec's art. For example, the top-hatted *flâneurs* gratifying their senses among the lower-class women, are sometimes cynical, sometimes impassive and sometimes lascivious. And yet these men were often modelled on Lautrec's friends who themselves engaged in such activity with relish, as did Lautrec himself. Images of this kind can be, and were, read as reproaches

HENRI DE TOULOUSE-LAUTREC
Portrait of Van Gogh
1887, Rijksmuseum Vincent
Van Gogh, Amsterdam

Pastel was an unusual medium for Lautrec, but the painting style he developed around this time combined both the linear hatching and the matt colouring apparent in

this portrait. Although Van Gogh and Lautrec were dissimilar in temperament, both were outsiders seeking self-fulfilment through art, and they shared both a responsiveness to new ideas and an avoidance of close affiliation with any particular group.

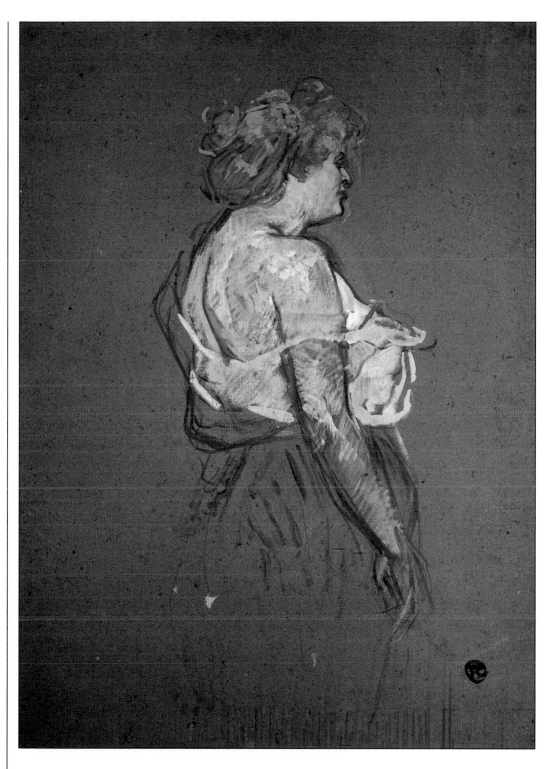

HENRI DE TOULOUSE-LAUTREC
Lucie Bellanger
1896, Musée Toulouse-Lautrec, Albi

This study of one of the prostitutes living in the brothel in the Rue des Moulins is a fine example of Lautrec's exploitation of the qualities of the thinned paint known as *peinture à l'essence*. This allowed him literally to draw in paint, so that despite the sketchy application of line and body colour, the result is convincing as a representation of three-dimensional form.

levelled against a social system that produced such inequalities, and Lautrec's sensitive treatment of prostitutes could be seen to support this view. But also his work was and still is characterized as non-judgemental — simply the Naturalist's straight presentation of assiduously collected facts. Neither view is quite adequate. In his paintings and drawings Lautrec presented his own intimate involvement, emotional and physical, in the way of life he depicted, showing us his comprehension of its pleasure and its pain.

New themes and last years

By about 1893 the focus of Lautrec's interests had begun to shift away from Montmartre towards central Paris, and his circle of friends and acquaintances broadened to include the well-known intellectuals and literary and political figures connected with the magazine *La Revue Blanche,* which stood for the most advanced ideas of the day. He began to be increasingly drawn to scenes of the theatre and popular operetta, which looked forward to a flurry of paintings based on Isidore de Lara's operetta

Messaline, painted in 1900, the year before he died.

By the mid-1890s Lautrec was at the height of his powers, and was now a well-known artist, having held several exhibitions and visited London, where he met Whistler and Oscar Wilde. Even the general public were aware of him through his posters. But his drinking, always excessive, was beginning to take its toll. He had become ill-tempered and was sometimes unintelligible, and by 1899 he was suffering so badly from DTs (delerium tremens) that he was forced to enter a sanatorium in an effort to cure his drinking problem. While there, determined to prove that he was fit to be released, he made a series of drawings of circus scenes, relying on his impressive visual memory.

The style he adopted in his final years, seen in paintings such as *At the Rat Mort* (see page 59), has perplexed some critics, being painterly and tonal rather than linear, as was his earlier work. The compositions are sometimes more complex (not always successfully) when compared with his earlier manner of focusing around a main — usually female — figure, and the colouring is more exotic and sumptuous. Some have seen this late manner as an attempt to redirect his art, while others have attributed the minimizing of line to his failing powers. Quite possibly both are correct. He had always been capable of uneven quality, but until the last few months when he could barely put brush to canvas, he could still produce paintings of real merit.

In spite of his stay at the sanatorium, Lautrec's extraordinary capacity for alcohol finally proved too much for a frame enfeebled since birth, and in 1901 his health gave out completely. He asked to be taken to his mother's home, and there he died, on 9 September, aged thirty-six. His last recorded words, spoken as he watched his father hovering by his bedside flicking flies from the coverlet with a piece of elastic drawn from his hunting boots, were "the old fool." Jules Renard, one of the writers he had met through *La Revue Blanche,* has left us a moving tribute to his character and his art: "The more one sees of him the taller he grows. In the end he assumes a stature above the average."

LAUTREC'S PAINTING METHODS

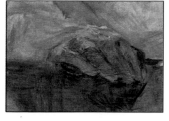

Lautrec's portrait of his mother, *The Comtesse Adèle de Toulouse-Lautrec,* shows an early use of his system of hatched brushstrokes.

Lucie Bellanger was painted on cardboard in *peinture à l'essence.* The thinned paint dries very fast, allowing the artist to use it almost as a drawing medium.

In *Jane Avril Dancing,* also on cardboard, Lautrec achieves an effect of transparency by overlaying layers of different-coloured brushstrokes.

Lautrec's early painting style was mainly derived from the Impressionists, but in his later works he developed a freer, more open technique, where fluid, graphic contours outlined blocks of more uniform colour, applied with rapid, bold sweeps of the brush. He often varied his brushstrokes, sometimes using dots, lines, hatching or zigzag marks to create a painterly equivalent for different surface textures.

He was greatly influenced by the subject matter and techniques of Degas, and both artists experimented with pigment heavily diluted with turpentine. This *peinture à l'essence,* as it is called, gives a matt effect that has something of the quality of pastel, quite unlike the buttery consistency and surface sheen of normal oil paint. Lautrec found that this fluid paint enabled him to "draw" with a brush, thus exploiting his genius for linear draughtsmanship. Degas used to drain the paints of oil by placing them on blotting paper, and both artists frequently painted on absorbent surfaces such as brown cardboard or unprimed canvas instead of the more usual pale- or white-primed support. Lautrec liked this kind of dull, muted ground colour, and preferred a palette of broken rather than pure hues, which suited the artificially lit indoor night scenes that he and Degas painted so often.

At the Rat Mort is an excellent example of Lautrec's characteristic thinly worked paint. It is painted on canvas, and shows how skilfully he was able to adapt the technique he had perfected when working on absorbent surfaces to the more conventional support. The canvas is a fine one with a pale commercial priming, and the colours used for the work were probably those shown below.

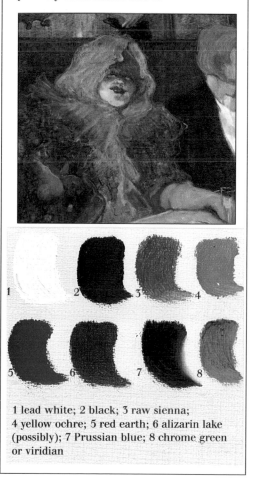

1 lead white; 2 black; 3 raw sienna; 4 yellow ochre; 5 red earth; 6 alizarin lake (possibly); 7 Prussian blue; 8 chrome green or viridian

CHRONOLOGY OF LAUTREC'S LIFE

1864   24 November: Lautrec born in the Hôtel du Bôsc at Albi.

1872   Attends the Lycée Fontanes, Paris.

1875   Poor health causes his mother to withdraw him from school for treatment.

1878-9   Fractures left and then right femur.

1880   Paints *Viaduct of Castel-Vieil at Albi*.

1881   Passes baccalauréat at second attempt. Subsequently concentrates on art, studying initially with René Princeteau. Paints *The Four-in-Hand* and *The Comtesse Adèle de Toulouse-Lautrec*.

1882   Enters the teaching atelier of Léon Bonnat and then that of Fernand Cormon, where he later becomes a friend of Emile Bernard and Van Gogh.

1885   Begins to frequent the dance-halls and bars of Montmartre. Becomes a friend of Aristide Bruant.

1886   Takes his own studio, 7 rue Touraque, which he retains until 1897. First publication of his drawings.

1887   Exhibits in several small exhibitions organized by Theo Van Gogh, the artist's brother. *Portrait of Van Gogh* painted at this time.

1888   Affairs with Suzanne Valadon and "Rosa Le Rouge" — contracts syphilis. February: exhibits with Les Vingt in Brussels.

1889   First exhibits at the Salon des Indépendents *(The Ball at The Moulin de la Galette)*. The Moulin Rouge opens; meets Jane Avril.

1891   Lautrec does drawings of the operations of Dr Péan. Becomes member of the hanging committee of the Salon des Indépendents. First poster commissioned by Zidler for The Moulin Rouge. Paints *A la Mie*.

The Ball at the Moulin de la Galette

Portrait of Paul Leclercq

Mme Poupoule at her Toilet

1892   Begins to paint brothel scenes and to publish colour lithographs. Paints *In Bed* and *Jane Avril Dancing*.

1893   Becomes involved with the journal *La Revue Blanche* and begins to use theatrical subjects. His first one-man show is organized by Joyant, but he opts to share it with Charles Maurin.

1894   Begins to stay for periods of time in brothels. Publishes the French series of Yvette Guilbert lithographs with preface by the critic Gustave Geffroy. Paints *Salon at the Rue des Moulins*.

1895   Meets Whistler and Wilde in London. Paints the booth panels for La Goulue. Travels to Lisbon with Maurice Guibert. Begins to frequent lesbian bars and publishes *Elles* series of lithographs.

1896   Alcoholism worsens. Holds one-man exhibition at the Manzi-Joyant gallery. Paints *Lucie Bellanger* and *Woman at her Toilet*.

1897   Moves to Rue Frochot, where he paints *Portrait of Paul Leclercq*.

1898   Exhibition at the London branch of Goupil's. Paints *Mme Poupoule at her Toilet*.

1899   Health deteriorates markedly during the winter. Is confined to a clinic at Neuilly between February and May, but by the year end is drinking again. Paints *At the Rat Mort*.

1900   Makes various trips. At Bordeaux becomes enthusiastic about the operetta *Messaline*.

1901   Returns briefly to Paris to put his studio in order. Has an attack of paralysis while at Taussat in August. Is taken by his mother to the family house at Malromé and dies there on 9 September.

THE PAINTINGS

THE COMTESSE ADELE DE TOULOUSE- LAUTREC

1881

36¼×31½in/92×80cm

Oil on canvas

Musée Toulouse-Lautrec, Albi

Lautrec's family could trace its ancestry and connections with the region around Albi in south-west France almost back to the time of Charlemagne. So illustrious a pedigree meant that Lautrec grew up in an atmosphere of wealth and privilege, aware that he was directly descended from a spirited race of warrior knights.

After the French Revolution such families survived with reduced political power. Lautrec's immediate forebears perpetuated a semblance of the chivalric code by devoting their lives largely to hunting of various sorts, and by showing an exaggerated disdain of useful work. In a period marked by one cause for political tension after another, Lautrec was fairly indifferent to politics, though he may have shared something of his family's rather forlorn monarchism.

Temperamentally his parents were ill-matched, though it is difficult to imagine what kind of woman could have lived harmoniously with Count Alphonse. They spent most of their married life apart. There was another son, but he died in 1868, leaving Lautrec as their only child. His upbringing was closely supervised by his mother, and since the bone disease that caused his legs to break was already apparent by the age of ten, he was withdrawn from school for treatment. His adolescence was thus a continuation of the life he had known as a child: a continual round of the family's various estates, later supplemented by visits to spas and clinics. Throughout his life he kept up an affectionate, if sometimes difficult, correspondence with his mother who, pious and reserved, was completely bewildered by both his art and his bohemian way of life.

In his early years he frequently did portraits of members of his family, estate workers, and people from his immediate circle of acquaintance. The picture's date of 1881 has been reasonably questioned on the grounds of its relatively advanced impressionistic style, but this is not necessarily attributable to any direct knowledge of Manet or Berthe Morisot with whose work it has been compared. Although not yet twenty, Lautrec had been visiting studios and exhibitions for a number of years. And although his comments in letters at this time suggest relatively conservative tastes in art, he could have picked up something of the "corrected and ameliorated Impressionism" that Zola noted in his review of the official Salon in 1880. Also, his earliest paintings, whether single figures either indoors or out, or the frequent horse subjects, conform to the same pattern as this — a fairly clarified main motif set within a vaguely sketched background.

There were fluctuations within his developing style, but the broad elements of his mature manner were already established before he undertook serious tuition with Bonnat in 1882. The half-length portrait, with the figure monumentally placed, was to remain throughout, one of the mainstays of his art. For example, in a painting of 1899, *The English Girl From The Star, Le Havre,* he used a system of differentiated hatching not unlike the rendering of stepped horizontals to the left of the figure in this portrait. Similarly, he continued throughout his brief career the device of situating a composition around an object or objects placed on a foreground surface, thus linking the spectator to the presence of the person observed.

Photographs of Lautrec's mother indicate a cast in the right eye, and in his various portraits of her he may have sought to minimize this feature by contriving poses requiring a downward gaze. Here the effect adds a sense of solemnity somewhat at odds with the pleasant airiness of the sunlit room, but apparently an accurate reflection of her character. Her resolve and moral rectitude could hardly have been in greater contrast to her husband's extravagant behaviour.

1

1 Lautrec's drawings at this time have a spikiness of line due to parallel- or cross-hatching, and his paintings show that his manner of applying pigment was to some extent a transcription of his graphic style. In the face of the countess, one of the most thoroughly worked areas of the painting, the method is not entirely successful — areas of light and shade fail to fuse together sufficiently and thus do not convey the smooth transition of form.

2 During the early 1880s Lautrec's most frequently used colour scheme was a range of cool greens and blues offset by touches of greater brilliance, usually red. This can be seen here, although the hues have been muted as befits the interior setting. His technique for conveying an impression of translucency was to undergo a number of modifications, but the juxtaposition of areas of contrasted hatchings was a device he returned to throughout his career.

3 *Actual size detail* Lautrec frequently arranged his portrait figures in relation to a foreground still life. It is typical of his approach to have combined the substantial clarity of such objects (and of faces and hands), with the airy vagueness of the rest of the canvas. By means of a relatively creamy application of paint he contrasts the lustrous glaze and rather bluish white of the cup and saucer with the softer white of the countess's dress, which in turn appears more brilliant amid the sombre tones surrounding it.

2

3 *Actual size detail*

THE BALL AT THE MOULIN
DE LA GALETTE

1889
$35\frac{1}{2} \times 39\frac{5}{8}$ in/90×100cm
Oil on canvas
Chicago Art Institute

Lautrec's boisterous personality and style masked a degree of uncertainty about his abilities as an artist. But by 1889 he was more secure in his commitment and consequently more ambitious in his compositions. Previously he had concentrated mainly on scenes involving movement and on portraits of single figures. Here he combines the two interests in a more complex organization which is nevertheless essentially a group of carefully arranged portraits. Subtly dominant is the painting's first owner, the bowler-hatted Joseph Albert, presented in surroundings which for Lautrec had become habitual — the dance-halls and café-concerts of Montmartre.

Albert was a friend and fellow painter, and it was he who introduced Lautrec to the organizers of the Salon des Indépendants in the autumn of this same year. *The Ball At the Moulin de la Galette* was one of three paintings Lautrec exhibited there. It betrays a hint of the stiltedness of the process of combining separately studied portraits within a relatively complex scheme, but there is a sense of being present; in effect the spectator assumes Lautrec's own seat at the table. "I work in my corner," he once said, meaning that he followed none of the current schools, but the statement applies equally well to his practice of detached observation.

The setting is the Moulin de la Galette, one of the increasing number of dance halls proliferating in Montmartre at the time. It was a less sumptuous venue, with a more down-at-heel clientele, than the Moulin Rouge, which opened for business the day after the exhibition closed, and which soon became Lautrec's favourite haunt. In the 1840s the poet Charles Baudelaire had begun to exhort artists to draw their subjects from modern life, and Manet, Degas and Renoir, among others, had exploited the potential of this kind of theme — one of Renoir's best-known paintings is of this same dance hall in the 1870s. Over a decade earlier, the Goncourt brothers had written about the novel possibilities of lighting and perspective to be had from theatre and ballet themes; the interesting compositional effect of viewing scenes, as it were, over the shoulders of foreground figures; and most important, the way that such devices could be a means of involving the spectator directly in the scene.

Above all, it was Degas whom Lautrec acknowledged in this approach to picture-making, both formally and in terms of subject matter — 1889 was the year the younger artist courted the older man's approval through a family of their mutual acquaintance, the Dihaus. Degas also frequently created a mood of isolated introspection in group portraits. Moreover, in the updating of Japanese spatial conventions in a European context, he provided the example that Lautrec was keenest to follow, so it is not surprising to see his influence in Lautrec's first really successful multiple figure composition.

In several earlier paintings Lautrec had used opposing diagonals as the basis of compositions, but never more daringly than here, where they form the principal structure by which he unites the more or less parallel friezes of foreground heads and background figures. Moreover it is one of these diagonals that draws attention to Albert, who is thrown into further prominence by his proximity to the most brilliant area of colour — the red hair of the woman seen from behind — in an otherwise fairly muted harmony of tones. One further trick is employed to link the two spatial planes together. The curiously unbalanced pile of saucers on the nearest table (signifying the number of drinks consumed) echoes the motion of the vigorously dancing couple swaying in the distance.

Degas's example was clearly important in this painting, but so too was Van Gogh's. After the brief period of serious tuition in the early 1880s, Lautrec's youthful exuberance of effect began to reassert itself, and Van Gogh, whom he had met at Cormon's *atelier*, evidently encouraged him in his development towards a personal style. In 1887 Lautrec did a pastel portrait of Van Gogh in an apparently characteristic pose (see page 12) and in a manner that suggests the influence of the Dutch painter's strongly directional brushwork and purity of colour.

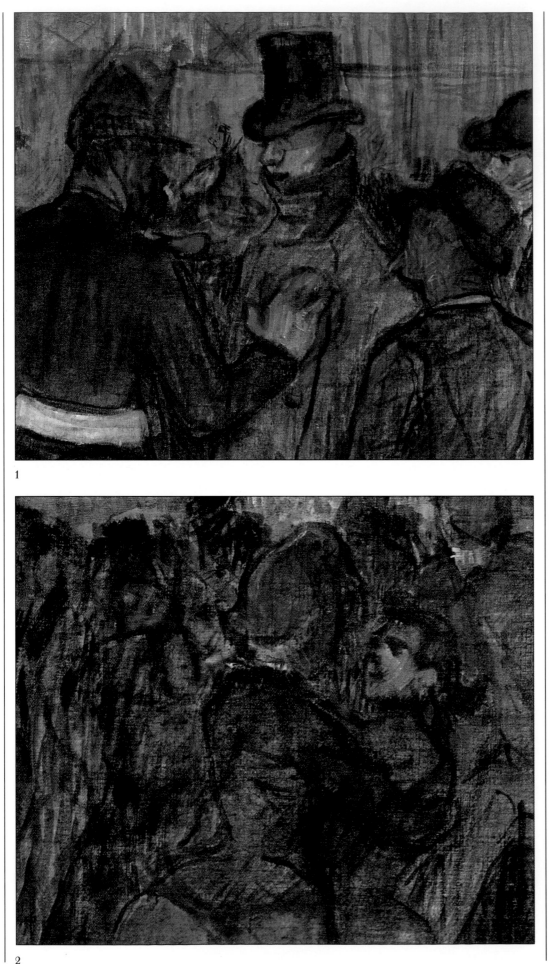

1

2

1 The frieze of background figures is made up of individualized types that emerge from the vague suggestion of a crowd beyond. With a few bold outlines their forms are broadly delineated with a brush lightly loaded with thinned paint. Body colour has also been applied thinly, and in places the weave of the canvas is scarcely covered, so that it becomes a neutral texture in its own right.

2 Perhaps naturally, Lautrec was keenly aware of physical differences in people, and here he has grouped three contrasting types of manhood. Although the painting bears traces of the sombreness of his period of academic training, it is also one of the earliest instances of his mature manner of applying thin paint in vertical overlaid strokes to an absorbent surface. He is reported to have been scathing about the traditional oil-painting method of creating luminosity by means of glazing. In some respects the method he adopted is closer to the transparency of watercolour.

3 This was Lautrec's first serious multiple figure composition, and typically, it combines his two major strengths, portraiture and the rendering of figures in motion. His colouring had become subdued while he was studying under Bonnat and Cormon, and the brilliance of the woman's red hair in an otherwise sombre-toned painting can be seen as a kind of emblem of his rebellion against such conservatism.

3

A La Mie

1891

$20^7/_8 \times 26^3/_4$ in / 53×68cm

Oil on cardboard

Museum of Fine Arts, Boston

As early as 1882 Lautrec had painted an alcoholic slumped in miserable reverie over his glass of wine, and towards the end of the decade he did a series of pictures of single young women similarly preoccupied, morose but attractive. These he gave titles borrowed from the songs of the entertainer Aristide Bruant — *A La Bastille, A Grenelle* — songs that stressed the individuality and humanity of prostitutes and the dehumanizing effect of their trade. In this painting he has placed two figures together, a device that he was to use frequently in subsequent works as it allowed him to exploit contrasting details of character. However, his use of it here is clearly a reference to Degas' *l'Absinthe* of c 1876, and the same mood of dejected *ennui* and isolation pervades both works.

But the circumstances in which the painting was produced raise questions about Lautrec's particular moral and artistic purposes. "This profession of conscientious policemen for the novel is assuredly the most abominable trade that an essentially aristocratic man can pursue." Thus Edmund de Goncourt described the mingled fascination and disgust experienced by the prosperous man-about-town recording the details of low-life — outwardly impassive yet inwardly intoxicated while "spying on the truth." Doubtless Lautrec shared this attitude to some extent, and yet he lacked both the reserve and the distaste implied by de Goncourt. By 1891 he was already known for his hard drinking. Maurice Guibert, who posed for the man, was a close friend of Lautrec's and a familiar *roué* in the bars of Montmartre. In July 1895 the journal *Fin de Siècle* reported that he was "of the whole capital the man who knew the prostitutes best." That same summer the two of them were sampling the brothels of Madrid.

Lautrec was not unusual in making use of photographs as *aides-memoire* to help the process of building a major composition. The photograph he used in this case reveals a number of calculated changes in the painting. Guibert's habitual good humour has been altered to a blend of ruefulness and cynicism. The transformation of the pretty young model is even more startling. Her expression has been coarsened and her physique altered, so that the right arm now hangs in limp resignation. The rendering of hands as an expression of character was especially important to Lautrec; it was one of the criteria he used to judge other artists. Here the mute drama of personalities evident in the faces is played out just as effectively in the contrast between Guibert's bony claw and the girl's bloated, loosened fist.

Victor Fournel had written of his desire "to look into the character indicated by a gait or physiognomy," and to discern "what series of virtues or of crimes have come to engrave an indelible and vivid expression on this or that face one is examining..." But like all pictorial artists seeking to convey a multiplicity of visual information in a seemingly momentary observation, Lautrec has had to, as it were, reverse this process, contriving both the psychological point of his scene and the spontaneity of its effect. The latter has been achieved in part by allowing the painting to retain the quality of a rapid sketch, though there is nothing rapid about the technique he employed to do this. It is painted with very much thinned oil colours on cardboard, the areas around the figures being built up by a variety of dabs, dashes and streaks which create a range of textural surfaces that throw the main motif into relief. This method is characteristic of Lautrec's mature manner, and the transparent effect it gives is very different from the loaded impasto used by Van Gogh. Nevertheless, the treatment of the regulated highlights on the woman's skirt is quite possibly due to the Dutchman's recent influence.

From the 1840s onwards the relation between photography and art had been a matter of controversy. Many artists opposed it as a threat, but others, notably Delacroix and Degas, responded positively and used photographs as an extension of the traditional process of preparatory drawings. Some of Lautrec's friends were photographers, Guibert included, and he occasionally used photographs in this way. The one that relates to this painting, however, is more than a peripheral study since, despite the changes he made in the finished painting, the whole scene has been calculated at the photographic stage. Interesting in this respect is the fact that rather than exploiting the medium for its capacity to capture transitory effects, Lautrec has contrived a static moment of self-reflection.

1

2

1 A photograph exists of the sitter, taken at much the same time as the painting. This shows how Lautrec deliberately aged the woman by altering and distorting her physique and features.

2 Foreground still lifes in Lautrec's paintings are always significant. They not only form a distinct element in the composition as a whole, but are also used as a device for involving the spectator in the scene. Sometimes, as here, they give a clue to the picture's meaning, which in this case he went to unusual lengths to contrive. Numerous writers have interpreted it as a portrayal of human degradation, but it could be argued that, like Lautrec himself, the pair, being daily confronted by the limitations of their separate fates, find solace only in alcohol and the company of similarly blighted souls.

3 *Actual size detail* The representation of hands was important to Lautrec as a means of conveying character, mood, psychological tension and so on. In contrast to the sketchiness of the dress and blouse the coarseness of her pink and swollen fingers has been emphasized by a precisely brushed-in outline. The left hand and right arm add to the woman's general air of dejection, while the right hand quietly suggests regret — both emotions combining in her facial expression. In places the paint has a pitted and chalky quality akin to pastel, a medium favoured by Degas, and which, like *peinture à l'essence,* produced matt colours without forfeiting intensity of hue.

3 *Actual size detail*

JANE AVRIL DANCING

1892

33×17⅜in/84×44cm

Oil on cardboard

Musée d'Orsay, Paris

Complex figurative compositions like *The Ball at the Moulin de la Galette* (see page 23) occur relatively infrequently in Lautrec's work. More typical is the presentation of a single character in a sketchily defined setting. His quick eye for the revealing outlines of people and animals in vigorous motion found a perfect subject in the wild gyrations of dancers. The popular craze for dancing had begun at least as early as the 1850s, and was an aspect of the official encouragement of organized leisure. Some of the more spectacular dancers achieved considerable popular fame and became the main attractions of dance halls such as Le Bal Mabille (operating in Paris before the full emergence of Montmartre as a centre for night-life in the 1880s).

Lautrec's adoption of both the theme and the dance hall itself is evidence of his rejection of the official routes to artistic prestige, and of his increasingly bohemian lifestyle. His involvement with the "minor" art of illustration is significant in this context. The first of the Montmartre cafés and cabarets he became identified with was Aristide Bruant's Le Mirliton, and in the mid-1880s he began to produce cover illustrations for the cabaret's journal of the same name. His subjects, in keeping with the sentiments of Bruant's satirical songs, were similar to the work of the singer's favourite artist, Steinlen, one of whose covers of 1886 featured the high kick of a can-can dancer.

During the 1890s, stimulated in part by the success of his posters, Lautrec began to specialize in similar subjects in his paintings, depicting the dancers and a widening range of café-concert entertainers. Jane Avril's career as a dancer began at the Moulin Rouge in the late 1880s, but like others who made their name in Montmartre — Lautrec included — she was soon taken up by the smarter establishments in central Paris, such as Le Décadents and Le Divan Japonais. The English poet Arthur Symons described her as a "fallen angel" with "an air of depraved virginity." Her refined and often melancholic manner set her apart from the brash vulgarity of the majority of dance-hall stars such as La Goulue (see page 43). She preferred to dance alone rather than as part of the sexually titillating ritual of the "naturalistic quadrille" or can-can, and her aloofness was resented by the other dancers. Lautrec's delight in individual female entertainers was usually of short duration, but his relationships with both Yvette Guilbert and Jane Avril were more lasting. Their intelligence and sensitive appreciation of his work formed the basis for a sustained friendship, and they occur frequently in his gallery of the personalities of the period. All his depictions of Jane Avril emphasize the withdrawn wistfulness of her features: for example, in the poster he made for her performances at the Jardin de Paris, he transformed the coquettish smile seen in her photograph into a blend of elegant hauteur and strained exertion. Like other artists of the period he often used photographs to supplement his sketches from life.

The sketch study for the painting (left) shows Lautrec's amazing ability to catch expressive movements in a few lines, suggesting not only the appearance of a figure in motion but also the personality. This required constant practice, and there are numerous accounts of how he perfected his drawing technique. When he was not satisfied with a sketch he would immediately discard it, repeating it over and over until he had achieved the result he sought. A comparison of the painting with the study indicates his desire to retain the vivacity of the latter and combine it, a little awkwardly perhaps, with a more fully realized portrait.

1

2

1 The man seen here is the same Englishman, Warrener, who featured that year in one of Lautrec's earliest colour lithographs (see page 9). He represents the type of man for whom the principal attraction of places like the Moulin Rouge was not so much the dancing as the possibility of picking up a woman.

2 Jane Avril's somewhat superior aloofness extended to her mode of dress: she alone among the dancers at the Moulin Rouge wore coloured petticoats and stockings, usually exotically combined pastel shades — in this case violet and dark purplish blue. Lautrec has built up this colour by hatching in some areas with the same aquamarine blue used as a background to the heads. The continuation of the blue in conjunction with greens and yellows shows his method of enlivening surfaces by means of a variety of systematically if speedily applied layers of directional strokes in harmonizing colours.

3 *Actual size detail*

3 *Actual size detail* Lautrec once complained of being criticized for not completing his pictures. "All I want to do is paint what I see. Anybody can finish off a painting." In this case however, some areas suggest he may have left it incomplete even by his standards, and it gives a valuable insight into his working methods. The head is the most fully realized part, the features being painted with precision, while the material of bodice and sleeves is sketchy. Lautrec has here exploited the possibilities of *peinture à l'essence*: an initial layer of white has been superimposed with further touches of consequently more substantial white, while elsewhere the cardboard shows through to stand for the colour of flesh beneath.

In Bed

1892
21¼×28in/54×71cm
Oil on cardboard
Musée d'Orsay, Paris

Lautrec began his practice of working in brothels (rather than simply visiting them) in 1892. Staying for more prolonged periods made him fully aware of the tedium and sadness of the prostitutes' lives — "servants of love," as he dubbed them. The result was a greater naturalism in his representations of the women and their daily routine. This quality is most marked in his sensitive treatment of their relationships with one another, formed in part to compensate for the lack of affection that was the natural consequence of their profession. They were surprised and charmed by the courteous attention he gave them, and no doubt his tragic deformity helped him to bypass some of the constraints on intimacy that would have been experienced by most normal men. Lautrec was thus allowed access to their privacy, making studies of them as they slept in the mornings, or during those moments when they were at complete ease with one another, in addition to when they went on display as objects of enticement awaiting purchase.

A comparison of this painting with Courbet's *Women Asleep* (opposite below), reveals much about their different intentions. The fact that Courbet's women are sleeping as well as naked renders them more open to voyeuristic interpretation, and this element was precisely the one demanded by Khalil Bey, the sedulous collector of high-class erotica, who commissioned the work. Moreover, Courbet himself is known to have attached special sexual significance to scenes of women asleep. Lautrec's painting, although like all his works the result of care-ful preparatory studies, has a chaste, fly-on-the-wall quality, quite different from the feeling Courbet gives of having furtively entered a bedroom. Usually when Lautrec tackled the theme of lesbianism he did show the women scantily clad, but even so they are emotionally involved rather than simply sexually preoccupied with each other. In this painting the warmth of mutual tenderness is conveyed almost entirely through the faces. The most striking contrast with the Courbet is the complete absence of glamour of the two tousled heads almost engulfed by the swelling folds of soft bedding. Lautrec once quipped of two women dancing together that they were "gazing into each other's eyes, even when they're closed." In this painting they are open — just — but the sentiment is the same.

It would be false to claim that Lautrec was not capable of producing ribald images of brothel life, but those that have survived destruction tend to be drawings or brief oil sketches rather than fully worked paintings. He also took pleasure, no doubt erotic, in arranging "sapphic occasions," but he made no moral judgements of lesbian practices, reserving his indignation for social hypocrisy. In the later 1890s when alcoholism began to exaggerate his fits of ill temper, his behaviour indignation was often justified. When a fashionable acquaintance, a man who himself made use of prostitutes, reproached Lautrec for residing in the brothels, he is reported to have shouted to the café at large, "I suppose you prefer to keep a brothel at home!"

GUSTAVE COURBET
Woman Asleep
1866, Musée de Petit Palais,
Paris

By the time Lautrec began to paint prostitutes, they had become for many French writers and artists both a symbol for the hypocrisy of modern society and a kind of parallel for the bohemian artist living on the fringe of respectability. For the majority of male painters, there were bound to be ambivalent associations of eroticism and/or repugnance, but Lautrec, because of his peculiar circumstances and temperament, was able to extend the intellectual interest in prostitutes by direct experience. His condition allowed him to empathize with their situation and thus to appreciate their humanity as distinct from their stereotype.

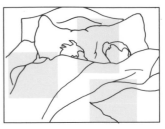

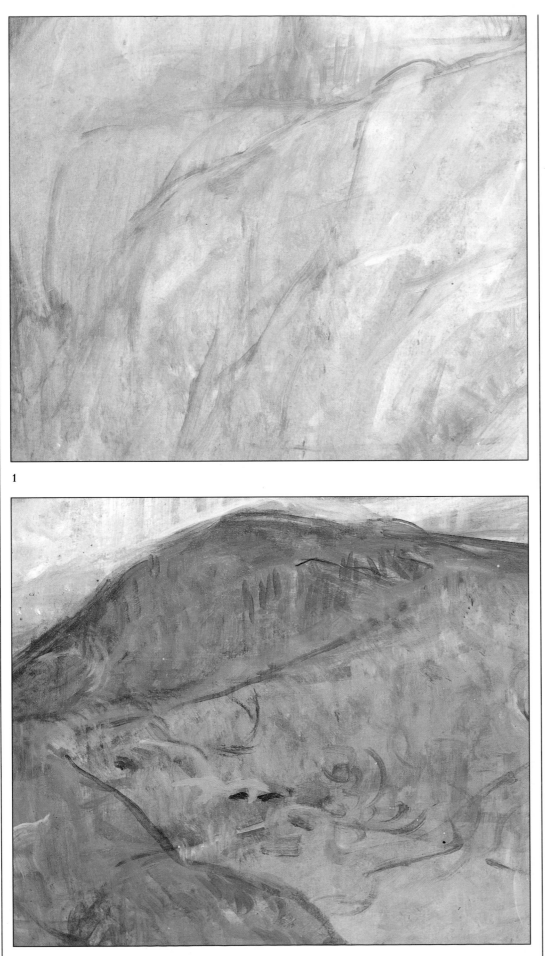

1

2

1 In his adaptation of the method of *peinture à l'essence*, Lautrec often made use of the soft amorphous texture of naturally speckled cardboard as a positive element in the finished picture. To different degrees it is visible in all three details illustrated here, and it becomes in effect a colour in its own right, close in hue to the faces and in tone to the dulled blues, greens and mauves of the shadows in the white sheets.

2 Compared with the more systematic brushstrokes in the upper right-hand corner or the thin parallel strokes of muted tones in the upper left, the application in this foreground area is more irregular, although the colour is more intense. To some extent this corresponds to the actuality of vision focused beyond the bedspread to the faces of the women.

3 *Actual size detail* This masterfully simple composition hinges on the relation of the two small heads set amid the billowing folds of the bedding. The two women are completely un-idealized — last night's rouge glows a little unnaturally on the otherwise cream areas of more brightly lit skin. But these tones, together with the blue highlights and red of the lips, are elaborated throughout the rest of the painting, and the colour scheme gives a wonderful impression of the warm morning light and the corresponding warmth of the woman's intimacy. In the faces themselves the colours are built up on top of one another within a structure of boldly applied brushed lines that create the forms of the heads and main features.

3 *Actual size detail*

THE SALON AT THE RUE DES MOULINS

1894
43³/₄×52¹/₈in/1.115×1.325m
Oil on canvas
Musée Toulouse-Lautrec, Albi

In 19th-century France, prostitution was regarded more or less as a social inevitability, and it was accepted as normal for adolescent males to visit brothels. Respectable opinion, however, was offended by public soliciting, so the pragmatic view was taken that it was better to allow prostitutes to practise in the privacy of brothels, known as *maisons de tolérance* or *maisons closes*. The policy never eradicated prostitution from the boulevards, bars and cafés, but in the 1880s and 90s there were renewed attempts at regulation. The question even developed into a point of general political controversy, both right- and left-wing opinion opposing such controls, the latter because the women were virtual prisoners in the brothels.

For the intellectual at the time, the prostitute had become something of a symbol of middle-class exploitation, and Naturalist writers such as Emile Zola frequently dealt with the theme. Lautrec's consistent use of it (often, paradoxically, as a source for subjects that stress the domestic normality of the women's daily lives) is in the same vein, but the regularity with which the theme continued to occur is another instance of his exploration of areas established by Degas. The latter's approach was on the whole more circumspect; his depictions of brothel life emphasized its sexual nature, but were usually on a relatively modest scale and in the more private media of the monotype print and drawings. His paintings of prostitutes are clothed women of the streets, while Lautrec's are more explicit, if curiously asexual.

The Salon at the Rue des Moulins was his largest and most ambitious treatment of the subject, the culmination of numerous related paintings and preparatory studies. This body of work was the result of the artist's habit of taking up residence for several days at a time in one of a succession of brothels — the one we see here was expensively decorated and catered for a variety of sexual tastes. Lautrec adopted this mode of life partly to gratify his own sexual needs and partly because he appreciated the general ambience — he called it, "prostitution palpitating." He complained about the stilted poses of professional models, finding more inspiration in the naturalness of these women who spent most of their time naked or semi-clad.

Lautrec's regular residence in brothels was also another aspect of the thorough and concerted manner in which he conducted his artistic investigations. He was initially secretive about his "lodgings," but in time began to parade the fact, giving 24 Rue des Moulins as his address, and even inviting the prestigious and slightly prudish dealer Paul Durand-Ruel to visit him there. However, when a representative exhibition of his work was held at the Manzi and Joyant gallery in 1896, his more obviously morally dubious paintings were kept in two locked rooms, Lautrec himself selecting those allowed access to them.

Sensitivity in such matters, even when sanctioned by the intellectual climate of Naturalism, is evidenced by the Irish writer George Moore's account of a conversation with Zola. A rivalry had gradually emerged between the relative merits of literature and art in their capacity to portray what Baudelaire called "the drama of modern life" effectively. When Zola asserted that no painters had achieved status comparable to some of the writers of the Naturalist school, Moore suggested the name of Degas. Zola retorted, "I cannot accept a man who shuts himself up all his life to draw a ballet girl as ranking co-equal in dignity and power with Flaubert, Daudet and Goncourt." Ballet girls in those days did not have the aura of respectability they have today, and Zola's opinion of someone shutting himself up with whores can readily be imagined.

In some ways this is one of Lautrec's most academic compositions. It hinges on the strength of the central column, around which he has asymmetrically arranged the figures of the women. Characteristically, one figure is dominant, and her nearness as well as the pale blue-whiteness of her clothing set against the rich harmonies created by derivatives of red, green and blue, makes her the focus of interest on which everything else depends. The diagonal emphasis of her striking posture is the major means by which foreground and background are linked. Lautrec's graphic work encouraged in him an appreciation of the positive value of negative spaces, and it is noticeable that the large open areas of the left foreground are treated more flatly than is usual in his work, an effect which adds to the almost tranquil mood of the scene.

One of the preparatory studies for the painting above

1 *Actual size detail*

1 *Actual size detail* Perhaps because of the complexity of the design, Lautrec emphasized more than usual the linear structure binding the composition as a whole. This can be seen especially in the woman in the foreground, the prostitute Mireille. Although based on numerous preparatory studies, this head, caught in half profile, retains the quality of a momentary observation. Dark outlines and a relatively even rendering of flesh indicate the tonal flattening of artificial lighting, and a similar approach is used for the areas of seating to her left.

2 The sumptuousness of the interior, with its shot-colour effects of plush and gilt, is rendered in part by the opposition of paired hues: reds with softened blues set against gold and greenish yellow (the latter like patina on bronze). Reds are prevalent, varying from touches of flaming intensity through to terracotta and dull pinks. The consequent luridness further adds to the air of artificiality by jarring with the dull orange Lautrec uses for all the women's hair.

3 The sketchiness of this area of the painting in one of Lautrec's most considered works indicates how, just as he directs attention to particular details, he can also direct it away from others. Compositionally, the picture is structured around a strong diagonal emphasis from the lower right-hand corner to the upper left, and then, through the direction of gaze of the three women in profile, across to the rearground right, to return, as it were to the spectator through the expressions of the two women detailed here.

2

3

LA GOULUE DANCING

1895
112¼ × 120¾ in / 285 × 307.5cm
Oil on canvas
Musée d'Orsay, Paris

Most of Lautrec's work is of a relatively modest size, but this is a very large canvas. He evidently relished this opportunity to work on a grander scale, even if the subject was not grand by academic standards. A photograph of about 1890 shows him at work in his studio, sitting near a huge ladder behind which is a commensurately large (but presumably lost) painting of a circus subject. The theme of this painting, which was commissioned by La Goulue herself, is similarly gaudy. The dancer, by this time turning to fat, had established her popular reputation as a specialist of the can-can and the "naturalistic quadrille" from which it derived. By the mid-1890s Lautrec's interest in Montmartre subject matter had diminished, but he responded with astonishing speed to La Goulue's curious request. Her letter arrived early in April and the panels (this painting and its companion piece) were installed by early June, her booth forming part of the annual Faire du Thrône at Neuilly. During this same period Lautrec, a confirmed anglophile, made a visit to England, which raises a number of interesting questions about the reasons for his inclusion of the recognizable portraits in the crowd of spectators. His visit to London coincided exactly with Oscar Wilde's scandalous trial, and by coincidence, he received the letter from La Goulue on the same day, 6 April, that Wilde was charged.

During Wilde's brief period of liberty on bail, Lautrec was introduced to him through their mutual friend, the artist Charles Conder. Wilde's by now flabby features can be recognized in the half profile of the figure slightly to the left of centre. His fictional presence at such an event seems incongruous. It would be pleasant to think that Lautrec was offering him an escape from the hue and cry of conventional morality, but the significance of his inclusion can perhaps be explained by the presence of another unlikely spectator, Félix Fénéon, the Anarchist and art critic, easily identifiable as the figure in the lower right-hand corner who had also recently been one of the central figures in a controversial trial and, like Wilde, had been briefly imprisoned. It would thus appear that Lautrec was courting irregular publicity on a bill-board scale by combining three distinctly different, but uniformly disreputable types: the slut, the homosexual and, by implication at least, the Anarchist agitator. Many of Wilde's friends abandoned him during the scandal, and he expressed his gratitude to Lautrec and Fénéon by including them in his list of those who were to receive presentation copies of his play *The Ideal Husband* when it was published in 1899.

La Goulue's fame and that of her partner Valentin le Desossé had been increased by one of Lautrec's most effective posters, and the extravagant movements of the pair formed the subject of another equally large painting. Together, the paintings formed the frontage of the fairground booth she performed in after leaving the Moulin Rouge in 1895. Her act by now featured belly-dancing in a cheaply oriental setting, but Lautrec has presented her giving the spectacular high kick with which she is said to have removed the hat of the Prince of Wales (the future Edward VII). Thus Lautrec has described both the origins of her career at the Elysée-Montmartre and its current phase, before she descended to performing with wild animals and eventually becoming a servant in a brothel. Both paintings are considerably faded. A writer for *La Vie Parisienne* referred to this one as "an unbelievable design in shrieking colours," and went on to note the irony of Wilde's inclusion, adding, "Oh, how good it is to see someone flouting the public!"

1

1 Lautrec enjoyed the ability of his friend Maurice Guibert to pull extraordinary faces, and his numerous depictions of him were rarely straightforward portraits. Here he has manipulated Guibert's features grotesquely to satirize what was most men's main pleasure while watching high-kicking dancers — a glimpse of naked thighs above dark stockings. By contrast he juxtaposes, perhaps ironically, the seemingly disapproving visage of another friend, the photographer (and womanizer) Paul Sescau.

2 According to contemporary accounts, the painting, done for a fairground booth, was far more garish in its original state. Though considerably larger in scale than most of Lautrec's paintings, it is typical of much of his work in that it is an arrangement of caricatures, the ones here being friends and acquaintances. The detail shows La Goulue's proud disdain, much commented on at the time, and the brilliantly rendered, animated figure of the pianist at the Moulin Rouge, M. Tinchant.

3 Perhaps the least exaggerated portrait in the painting is the one shown here, of the Anarchist writer and Symbolist critic Félix Fénéon. Possibly his habitual appearance was eccentric enough to require little distortion. Lautrec delighted in depicting physical contrasts, between the irregular outlines of Fénéon's profile and the similarly extravagant silhouette of Jane Avril he has placed the simpler, rounded shapes of his own diminutive and slope-shouldered frame.

2

3

WOMAN AT HER TOILET

1896
25¼×20½in/64×52cm
Oil on cardboard
Musée d'Orsay, Paris

From time to time throughout his career, Lautrec produced series of what he called "impositions." Some of these exercises in self-imposed discipline seem to have been motivated by a desire to improve his technical skills along lines that were to some extent at variance with his facility of draughtsmanship. This, although masterly in its way, often veered towards caricature or exaggeration, whether of face or figure. His results were usually convincing as representations of the seen world because of his ability to capture the fundamentals of character or movement with an expressive line that suggested substantiality of form rather than describing it literally.

The accurate representation of spatial depth had posed a technical problem to Western artists since the time of Giotto, but by the 1890s many of Lautrec's contemporaries, notably Bernard and Gauguin, were rejecting traditional Western perspective. They were producing paintings that tended to flatten form, emphasize linear outline and controvert naturalistic vision by using large areas of unbroken or slightly textured colour. Such methods, derived in modified form from the two-dimensional art of the Japanese print, had the combined effect of minimizing spatial recession and stressing surface pattern in a more abstract way. Lautrec, encouraged by his early recognition as one of the most spectacular of contemporary graphic artists, often employed spatial metaphors that implied the space of an environment without actualizing it.

The succession of paintings and drawings of nude or semi-nude women, of which this is one of the best and most typical examples, can be seen as a calculated attempt on Lautrec's part to counter-balance the non-naturalistic tendencies in his art. Adopting an elevated viewpoint like this one, cutting off objects at the picture edge, and laying one object behind another in surprising juxtapositions was obviously an extension of the lessons learned from Japanese artists. But these compositional devices are also another example of Lautrec's debt to Degas, particularly his late pastels of intimately observed nudes, such as *The Tub* of 1886. But there is an important difference — which interestingly stands in contrast to Lautrec's more characteristic work: whereas part of Degas's purpose was to show his women in some kind of self-absorbing activity, Lautrec's model here is quite evidently posing. Seen in abstract terms, her whole arrangement is organized to give a physical sense of a head poised above the conical structure of the body.

A further point of dissimilarity between the two artists is their respective approaches to the modelling of the flesh and its substructure of bone and muscle. Degas does this by means of the subtle diffusion of light, but Lautrec's manner had never been delicate, and his modulation of tones and colours was always as brash as his line was feelingly sensitive. There is much of this fine linear quality here, seen in the irregularities of contour provided by the oblique and downward viewpoint, and not surprisingly, it is in this respect that the painting succeeds best.

Many of the women Lautrec painted, whether recognizable or anonymous, had red or reddish hair. Perhaps significantly, examples begin to occur in his paintings around 1888, when he is known to have had an affair with a woman called, appropriately, Rosa La Rouge. Oddly, given his fascination with facial character, the view he often took of his models was from behind. It may be no more than coincidence, but among the many anecdotes that attach to his name, is one concerning a young woman who had to hold back her tears because he asked if he could sit behind her while they talked. His physical appearance was inescapable.

1 *Actual size detail*

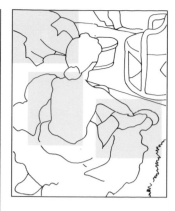

1 *Actual size detail* The picture was one of a series of exercises in self-instruction, and it betrays some strain due to the technical achievements Lautrec was seeking to acquire. For the successful representation of flesh tones, his characteristically bravura handling had always depended on the painting being seen at a certain distance so that boldly juxtaposed and overlaid strokes of varied colours could blend together in the eye. However, a detail such as this demonstrates the limitations of this manner, especially when compared with the similar nudes of Degas, which this picture emulates.

2 In another series of "impositions," Lautrec had studied single women in the garden of a friend. In those one might have expected him to pay greater attention to the play of light on the scene as a whole, but instead the backgrounds were treated with brevity as though to serve as a vague adjunct to his principal interest, the human figure. Often this approach was successful, but here, where a definite attempt has been made to render a solidly three-dimensional body in space, the result is not quite convincing. With lines of various pastel colours he has impatiently enlivened the drapery lying on a briefly defined wicker chair.

3 The definition of solid form principally by line is most apparent in the relation of the arm to the leg, and of both to the whole. The detail shows the deceptively simple means by which this was effected.

2

3

PORTRAIT OF PAUL LECLERCQ

1897
21¼×25⅛in/54×64cm
Oil on cardboard
Musée d'Orsay, Paris

The poet André Rivoire, who was painted by Lautrec in 1901, the year of the artist's death, published shortly afterwards an account of Lautrec's approach to portraiture. He stressed the importance of getting to know the sitter as part of the sometimes lengthy process of gestation culminating in rapid fruition. "... Two or three sittings, sometimes only one, were enough for him ... To appreciate the extraordinary sureness of touch one must have watched him at work on a canvas or a sheet of cardboard ..." Before commencing on the whole painting, Lautrec would sometimes distract himself with some detail in a corner before launching with great speed into the portrait. Rivoire tells us that "... his work was there, all ready in front of him; his eyes could visualize it in its complete form on the canvas as if it existed there beforehand; he seemed to be tracing over invisible lines. He would sing, laugh and chat like a common workman over his task ... Very rarely ... one became aware of a more minute attention."

This account seems to be at variance with what is known of Lautrec's reduced mental and physical condition at this time. Maurice Joyant, who took over the branch of Goupil's gallery from Theo Van Gogh after the latter's premature death in 1891, recorded some seventy-five sittings for his portrait, done a few months earlier than Rivoire's — and Lautrec had been a close friend of his since childhood. However, Rivoire's account, though a little idealized, is probably a reasonable description of Lautrec's methods before the debilitating effects of his alcoholism began to seriously affect his dexterity.

Lautrec himself termed the process, "the technique of leading up," and it tallies with Paul Leclercq's account of the portrait shown here. Leclercq, also a poet, was the founder of the literary and artistic journal *La Revue Blanche* in 1889, and he and Lautrec became friendly in about 1894. According to his account, the portrait of three years later was done over a period of about four to five weeks, though he added that he probably only sat for two or three hours. He noted that Lautrec wore a large floppy hat, in order, as Lautrec put it, "... to concentrate the light and avoid shadows ..." Habitually energetic, Lautrec might daub only a couple of strokes before breaking into some vulgar ballad and then jumping up to lead Leclercq off to a bar.

The painting is an unusual one for Lautrec, who seldom engaged the viewer so directly in his portraits, whether formal or informal. When he did so, as here, the results were often striking psychological penetrations of character. This is one of the finest examples, not least because of the slightly unnerving sensation it gives of being observed by the sitter while at the same time observing him.

Lautrec's connections with *La Revue Blanche* from 1893 onwards raised the intellectual level of his immediate social circle. From 1891 Leclercq and the brothers Thadée and Alexandre Natanson shared control of the journal's advanced editorial policy, and through them Lautrec was introduced to a wider range of writers and artists, especially the group known as the Nabis, who followed Gauguin's advice to paint in flat, pure colours. One of the writers was the Anarchist Félix Fénéon who, after his trial, in which he was successfully defended by Thadée Natanson, became an assistant editor of the journal. However, Lautrec did not abandon his former habits. Another writer, Romain Coolus, may have been responsible for his increasing interest in theatrical subjects (see page 14), but Lautrec drew Coolus into his old life by inviting the latter to join him in his extended stays in brothels. Also, as Leclercq noted, Lautrec seemed more interested in the theatrical ambience and the audience than in the plays; his depictions were a continuation of his interest in performers rather than in the interpretation of a text.

A comparison of the portrait of Leclercq with that of the prostitute in *Mme Poupoule at her Toilet* (see page 55), of about the same time, shows how he could adapt the main features of his style to suit different situations or personalities. The predominance here of soft vertical striations in a harmony of mainly blues and greens creates an air of refined tranquility around the figure. It is a good example of the atmospheric possibilities Lautrec could achieve with thinned oil paint applied to absorbent cardboard. This technique, known as *peinture à l'essence,* which Lautrec adapted from the methods of Degas and Raffaëli, allowed him to overlay lines or webs of different colours to build up a sense of luminosity without resorting to normal *chiaroscuro* methods to depict dark areas and shadows.

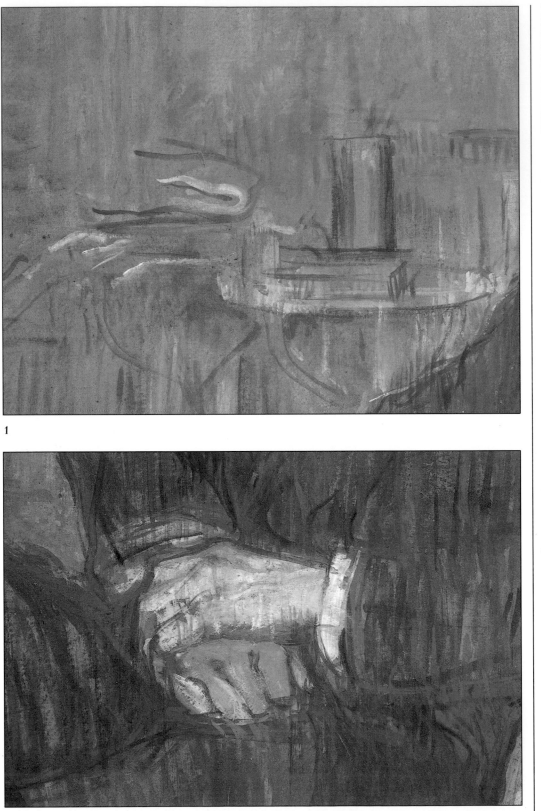

1

2

1 Details in the backgrounds of Lautrec's portraits are often most effective when most simple, and thus less likely to interfere with the main motif. Here an atmosphere of cool luminosity is created by the combination of aqueous blues and greens, within which the tables and their contents shimmer with a translucency that is both fragmented and substantial.

2 A curious aspect of Lautrec's portraiture is that the paintings as a whole can successfully survive occasional weaknesses of one or more of the parts — here Leclercq's right arm and leg. The success of these portraits is partly due to Lautrec's caricaturist's instinct for a convincing overall posture and partly to the care he took over the dominant elements of head and hands and their placing in relation to the fundamental lines of the composition.

3 *Actual size detail* In his later work Lautrec frequently used a dark blue outline to lay out the basic concept of the figure in its setting. Just how rudimentary this was can be clearly seen here. The detail also reveals the use of the tone of the cardboard support as a lightening element, as well as Lautrec's application of vertical textures. The face is much more thoroughly modelled, and the way the head is tilted to one side adds to the intensity of the gaze.

3 *Actual size detail*

MME POUPOULE AT HER TOILET

1898

24×19½in/60.8×49.6cm

Oil on wood

Musée Toulouse-Lautrec, Albi

Lautrec's close contact with *La Revue Blanche* led to friendship with some of the painters of the Nabis group (which included Bonnard and Vuillard), who were helped and promoted by the journal. There are hilarious accounts of a spectacular party held by the Natansons to celebrate the completion of a series of panels by Vuillard at which Lautrec devastated the company by his near-lethal skills as a mixer of cocktails.

The rich colouring and texturing of the background of this painting shows some similarity with Vuillard, who worked up his scenes of domestic interiors with an almost claustrophobic accumulation of decorative surfaces. However, it is clearly a continuation of Lautrec's own thematic interests and stylistic development. As in the early portrait of his mother (see page 19) the observer is placed in close proximity to the self-absorbed sitter via the top of an intervening table on which is a carefully arranged and sensuously painted still life.

Madame Poupoule was a prostitute Lautrec painted a number of times during this period. By the late 1890s, his persistently naturalistic approach was becoming old-fashioned in avant-garde terms, but the theme of prostitutes, which continued to play a crucial role in his art and life, was still popular with writers and the reading public. Two years earlier, for example, he had considered illustrating Edmond de Goncourt's *La Fille Elisa,* published twenty years earlier. Pierre Loüy's *Aphrodite* of 1896 was a paean in praise of prostitution and sold 125,000 copies by 1904. But this is far less obviously a painting of a whore than the earlier brothel paintings, indeed on one level it is simply a private portrait of a woman combing her hair. Lautrec's deformity denied him the kind of conjugal intimacy taken for granted by normal men, but he could enjoy something of the same closeness with women of this kind.

Scenes such as this were common in Degas' work, and it was always to Degas that Lautrec looked for guidance, stylistic, technical and iconographic. Degas' opinion of his paintings mattered to Lautrec more than anyone else's, and to judge from the older artist's recorded statements, that opinion was somewhat equivocal. After silently perusing the works on show at Lautrec's first major exhibition, at the Boussod and Valadon Gallery in 1893, he is said to have called out on leaving, "One can see, Lautrec, that you know the ropes." Possibly from a lack of confidence, Lautrec had asked to share this exhibition with a now little-known painter, Charles Maurin. It thus is ironic that Degas subsequently advised a patron who was considering buying Lautrecs to buy Maurins instead. "Lautrec has a good deal of talent," he said, "but he is merely the painter of a period . . ." Other reported comments indicate irritation at being so closely followed, and in a manner he probably considered too flagrantly immoral. Years after Lautrec's death he said of Lautrec's work as a whole that "It all stinks of the pox." However, if an incident described by another contemporary is true, he could also be enthusiastically encouraging. The story is that Lautrec and some others encountered Degas in the street on his way back from Durand-Ruel's, where he had been looking at examples of Lautrec's work. Degas praised him at length, concluding, "Work hard! You've got a splendid talent." As he and his friends walked on, Lautrec, visibly shaken, asked whether Degas could possibly have meant it, and one of them crushed him cruelly by asserting that he had been made a fool of. This seems unlikely; although Degas could be unkind and ill-tempered he was known for biting sarcasm rather than for malicious guile. The anecdote is interesting in another way, however, as it provides one of the numerous instances of Lautrec's uncertainty as to the lasting qualities of his art.

A comparison with Degas's depictions of woman combing their hair reveals both the similarities and differences in their respective approaches. There is the same sense of invaded privacy and of surreptitious access to an exclusively feminine ambience. But Degas was principally concerned with achieving effects of momentary, glimpsed movement so that the faces, though often clearly visible, indicate little of personality beyond an almost animal lack of self-consciousness. Lautrec on the other hand manipulates every facet of the painting to concentrate on the woman's character in a moment of introspection. In this sense he comes closer to the similar representations of the American Impressionist Mary Cassatt.

1 *Actual size detail*

1 *Actual size detail* Mme Poupoule is caught literally in a moment of self-reflection while combing her hair. The positioning of the hands adds to the pervading sense of stillness and the serious thoughtfulness of the expression on her only partially visible face.

2 Lautrec here uses another device learned early in his career, one borrowed from another artist, Jean Louis Forain, whose speciality was the representation of objects in dimly lit interiors by means of a few deft strokes of highlight. The more than usually claustrophobic feeling of this work also invites comparison with the treatment of similar subjects by Vuillard, but while the latter almost overwhelms his figures by the decorative treatment of wall, floor coverings, and so on, Lautrec's colours seem to create a sense of amorphous depth.

3 Although the head and hands are the main area of psychological interest, Lautrec has here set up a foreground motif which is of almost equal importance. The colouring of the jar and lid is more substantial, because more intense in hue, than any other area of the picture, being a more saturated variant of the colour of the girl's hair. Similarly solid in volume, although transparent, are the squat bottles near the mirror, and the physical presence of these objects is enhanced by the echoes of shimmering white highlights on the cloth.

2

3

AT THE RAT MORT

(The Tête à Tête Supper)
1899
$21^5/_8 \times 18^1/_8$in/55×46cm
Oil on canvas
Courtauld Institute Galleries, London

The painter William Rothenstein, who documented the artistic life of the period on both sides of the Channel, wrote of this restaurant, where he was first introduced to Lautrec, as follows. "The Rat Mort by night had a somewhat doubtful reputation, but during the day was frequented by painters and poets. As a matter of fact it was a notorious centre of lesbianism, a matter of which, being very young, and a novice to Paris, I knew nothing. But this gave additional attraction to Conder and Lautrec." He went on to comment on the lesbian and brothel themes Lautrec was already known for (see page 39), adding, "Nor can I imagine anyone else ready to face what Lautrec did in order to get material for his studies."

Earlier in the decade, when staying for periods of time in brothels, Lautrec had been attracted by the affection some of the women could display to one another. The series of lithographs he published as an album in 1896, entitled *Elles,* was for long believed to represent domestic life in the brothels, but it is now thought more likely that the theme is the daily lives of two particular women, only occasionally engaged in prostitution. Montmartre had attracted a number of lesbian bars, and Lautrec began to frequent them in the mid-1890s. Among these were Le Hanneton in the Rue Pigalle and La Souris in the rue Breda, where he began to stay from time to time. Thadée Natanson thought that he was drawn to lesbians because, "they love each other more deeply than men can love them." No doubt a further attraction was that he relished entering places where normal men were shunned, while he was welcomed.

Natanson also observed that Lautrec's eyes now shone less brightly, outdone by the glints of his pince-nez. By 1898 his drinking had become even more prodigious, and he no longer seemed to care if it rendered him publicly unconscious. Francis Jourdain was sad to see him at La Souris asleep and dribbling. To others he seemed to be bent on self-destruction; friends noted that his enthusiasm for enticing subjects and even for painting itself was on the wane. Delirium tremens and the breakdown of his health that led to his death was only months away. And yet he was still painting and sometimes producing works that stand comparison with anything he had ever done.

The format of this painting is similar to that of *Mme Poupoule* (see page 55), but the mood could hardly be more different, and the style seems accordingly changed. Moreover, coming so soon after the almost hallucinatory precision of the circus drawings Lautrec had done in the sanatorium at Neuilly, the breadth of handling is remarkable. After about six months abstinence he was drinking again, and some have seen this late manner as the result of a reduced ability to control the line on which his art had always depended. But although it is true that his faculties were greatly impaired, the painting can be seen in a different way. The contrast between the two works suggests that Lautrec might have been consciously taking further a trend that had been evident in his earlier work, and was exploring an idea that had been current for at least a generation, namely that colour, tone and even the type of brushstroke used should be in harmony with the psychological content of a picture. Here the pie-eyed smiling face of the courtesan Lucy Jourdan is set amid the swaying forms and Baroque rhythms that convey the rolling pleasure of her inebriation.

According to contemporaries, Lautrec was only minimally interested in art theory. Technique was a much more engaging preoccupation, whether the term was applied to art or the difficult business of mounting a bar stool. *Technique des Vénétiens* was a frequent expression, and by this he meant a preference for sumptuous colour and loose handling as against line, the Florentine and academic preference. Louis Anquetin, a friend who had also trained at Cormon's *atelier*, was also interested in the Baroque tradition and its 19th-century derivatives. *At the Rat Mort* suggests that Lautrec may also have been prepared to take the side of Venetian painting and the freedom of such artists as Rubens and Delacroix against the linear emphasis of Poussin and Ingres.

1 *Actual size detail*

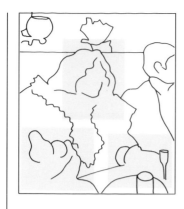

1 *Actual size detail* Lautrec excelled in the representation of people in artificial light. His bold technique lent itself well, as here, to the stark demarcation of shaded and illumined areas of the face. With virtually a single stroke of contrasting colour he underscores each eye, while the luscious red fullness of the mouth is a concentration of the flourishes and colouring that permeate the whole painting.

2 Always careful in the placing of foreground objects in relation to the figure beyond, Lautrec has here made humorous use of the shape of the pear as a kind of miniature in reverse of the head with its extravagant top-knot of hair. The fruit and bowl have been painted more thickly than her clothing beyond, where the canvas weave is clearly apparent.

3 The cool bluish grey of the woman's gloved hand is echoed throughout the composition. It appears in the glasses and on the wall behind the woman's head, and continues in the exhilarating cascades of her transparent collar and pale blonde hair. This relatively neutral tone is combined with touches of equally muted green, and these colours, when set against the areas of deep red, appear stronger in hue, contributing to the air of sensuality.

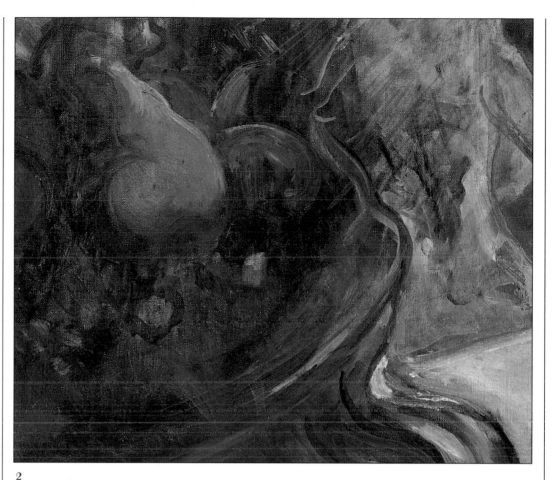

2

3

PHOTOGRAPHIC CREDITS
The photographs in this book were provided by the following:
APF, Paris 6; The Art Institute of Chicago 23-25; Bridgeman Art
Library, London 11, 35 bottom; British Museum, London 10 bottom;
Courtauld Institute Galleries, London 15 bottom, 59-61; Hubert Josse,
Paris 7-13, 14 bottom, 15, 19-21, 31 right, 32-33, 35 top, 36-37, 39-41,
43-45, 47-49, 51-53, 55-57; Museum of Fine Arts, Boston 27-29; Hans
Petersen, Copenhagen 14 top; Vincent Van Gogh Foundation/National
Museum Vincent Van Gogh, Amsterdam 12.